Presented to:

Emma

From:

Elizabeth & Locke

Date:

Christmas 2002

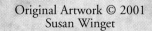

Text Copyright © 2001
The Brownlow Corporation
6309 Airport Freeway, Fort Worth, Texas 76117

Written and compiled by Anne Buchanan
Illustrated by Susan Winget
Designed by Lakeside Design

ACKNOWLEDGEMENTS:

The Martin Luther Christmas Book, trans. and arranged by Roland H. Bainton.
(Philadelphia: Westminster, 1948).

The Prophetic Imagination, Walter Breuggemann. (Minneapolis: Fortress Press, 1978).

Christmas Song. Elizabeth Buchanan. ©1997. Used by permission.

Incident at the Manger. C. W. Christian. ©2001. Used by permission.

Family Celebrations for Christmas, Ann Hibbard. (Grand Rapids: Baker, 1993).

The Mood of Christmas, Howard Thurman. (Friends United Press, 1985).

Sing to the Lord: Devotions for Advent, Mary Anna Vidakovich.
(Nashville: The Upper Room, 1994).

The Vigil: Keeping Watch in the Season of Christ's Coming, Wendy M. Wright.
(Nashville: The Upper Room, 1992).

ISBN: 1-57051-850-5
Printed in The United States of America

O HOLY NIGHT

Written and Compiled by:
Anne Buchanan

Illustrated by:
Susan Winget

Brownlow

The First Noël

This was how the birth of Jesus Christ took place. His mother Mary was engaged to Joseph, but before they were married, she found out that she was going to have a baby by the Holy Spirit. Joseph was a man who always did what was right, but he did not want to disgrace Mary publicly; so he made plans to break the engagement privately. While he was thinking about this, an angel of the Lord appeared to him in a dream and said,

"Joseph, descendant of David, do not be afraid to take Mary to be your wife. For it is by the Holy Spirit that she has conceived. She will have a son, and you will name him Jesus —because he will save his people from their sins."

…So when Joseph woke up, he married Mary, as the angel of the Lord had told him to. But he had no sexual relations with her before she gave birth to her son. And Joseph named him Jesus.

—*Matthew 1:18–24, TEV*

A Girl Named Mary

For this how wondrously he wrought!
A maid in lowly human place
became in ways beyond all thought,
the chosen vessel of his grace.

—*Caelius Sedulius*

Mary truly wondered at [the angel's] words.
We must recall that she was human and
did not know and understand everything.
All that had happened was as incredible
to her as to anyone else.
NEVERTHELESS, SHE BELIEVED,
AND SO MUST WE ALL.

—*Martin Luther*
Translated by Roland H. Bainton

A Man Named Joseph

*M*ost likely, Joseph had never imagined
that he would be the stepfather of the Messiah.
Yet here comes the angel of the Lord,
asking Joseph to believe something unbelievable!
How do we know that Joseph believed the angel? Because
"when Joseph woke up he did what the angel
of the Lord had commanded him…"

Often God calls us to believe the unbelievable
and do the impossible. How can we do this?
We must simply take God at his word, as Joseph did,
and then immediately obey. If, every day, we
listen to God's Word and obey it without hesitation,
we, like Joseph will be ready for his coming.

—*Ann Hibbard*

*W*hen the wonder and majesty of the season
seems submerged in the vacuous and pain-filled realities
of everyday life, I like to think of Joseph
Not as the idealized patriarch of the Holy Family,
but as the overlooked figure in the
Advent and Christmas story....
Joseph represents for me the hidden, loving involvement
in family that comes from both men and women,
that is neither obviously rewarding nor visible....
Joseph is balancing the budget one more time,
clipping out coupons, and reheating or disguising
the leftovers in one more casserole surprise....
Joseph is shouldering college tuition costs
or giving Saturdays to coach the softball team....
For it is against this backdrop of stability and unflagging care
...that the miracle of the divine birth is given
a place to grow and mature.

—*Wendy M. Wright*

A Child is Born

AT THAT TIME Emperor Augustus ordered a census to be taken throughout the Roman Empire. When this first census took place, Quirinius was the governor of Syria. Everyone, then, went to register himself, each to his own home town. Joseph went from the town of Nazareth in Galilee to the town of Bethlehem in Judea, the birthplace of King David. Joseph went there because he was a descendant of David. He went to register with Mary, who was promised in marriage to him. Mary…was pregnant, and while they were in Bethlehem, the time came for her to have her baby. She gave birth to her first son, wrapped him in cloths and laid him in a manger—there was no room for them to stay in the inn.

—*Luke 2:1–7*

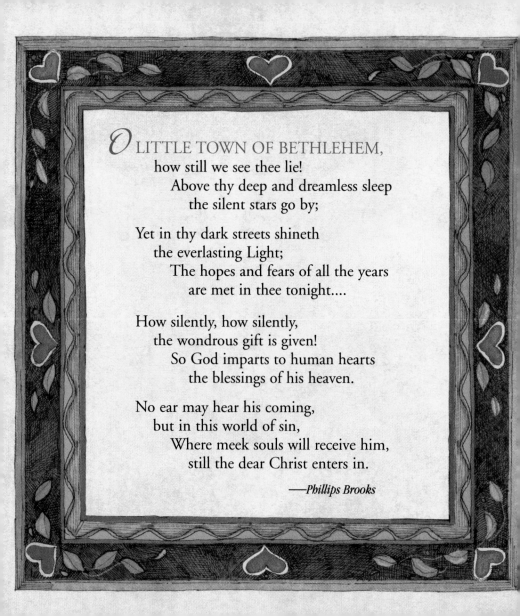

O LITTLE TOWN OF BETHLEHEM,
how still we see thee lie!
Above thy deep and dreamless sleep
the silent stars go by;

Yet in thy dark streets shineth
the everlasting Light;
The hopes and fears of all the years
are met in thee tonight....

How silently, how silently,
the wondrous gift is given!
So God imparts to human hearts
the blessings of his heaven.

No ear may hear his coming,
but in this world of sin,
Where meek souls will receive him,
still the dear Christ enters in.

—Phillips Brooks

The Birth of Wonder

*F*all on your knees!

O hear the angel voices! O night divine!

O night when Christ was born. O night divine!

O night, O night divine!

GOOD MAN JOSEPH TOILED
THROUGH THE SNOW—
SAW THE STAR O'ER THE STABLE LOW;
MARY SHE MIGHT NOT FURTHER GO—
WELCOME THATCH AND LITTER BELOW!
JOY WAS HERS IN THE MORNING.

—Kenneth Grahame

Christmas Prayer

O GOD, OUR LOVING FATHER,
help us rightly to remember the birth of Jesus,
that we may share in the song of the angels,
the gladness of the shepherds,
and the worship of the Wise Men.
May the Christmas morning
make us happy to be your children
and the Christmas evening bring us to our bed
with grateful thoughts, forgiving and forgiven,
for Jesus' sake. Amen.

—*Robert Louis Stevenson*

GIVE THANKS TO THE LORD, FOR HE IS GOOD; HIS LOVE ENDURES FOREVER.

—*Psalm 107:1*

The Other Wise Man

Far over the eastern plain a white mist stretched like a lake. But where the distant peak of Zagros serrated the western horizon the sky was clear. Jupiter and Saturn rolled together like drops of lambent flame about to blend in one.

As Artaban watched them, behold! An azure spark was born out of the darkness beneath, rounding itself with purple splendors to a crimson sphere, and spiring upward through rays of saffron and orange into a point of white radiance. Tiny and infinitely remote, yet perfect in every part, it pulsated in the enormous vault as if the three jewels in the Magian's breast had mingled and been transformed into a living heart of light. He bowed his head. He covered his brow with his hands. "It is the sign," he said. "THE KING IS COMING, AND I WILL GO TO MEET HIM."

—*Henry Van Dyke*

The night is the long night,
It will snow and it will drift,
White snow there will be till day,
White moon there will be till morn,
This night is the eve of the Great Nativity,
This night is born Mary Virgin's Son,
This night is born Jesus, Son of the King of glory,
This night is born to us the root of our joy,
This night gleamed the sun of the mountains high,
This night gleamed sea and shore together,
This night was born Christ the King of greatness,
Ere it was heard that the Glory was come,
Heard was the wave upon the strand,
Ere 'twas heard that His foot had reached the earth,
Heard was the song of the angels glorious,
This night is the long night.

—*Traditional Gaelic*

When Heaven Came to Earth

*A*ll Wonders in one sight! Eternity shut in a span.
Summer in winter, day in night,
Heaven in earth, and God in man.
Great little one! whose all-embracing birth
Lifts earth to heaven, stoops heav'n to earth!

—*Richard Crashaw*

Starlight

O FATHER, may that Holy star
Grow every year more bright,
And send its glorious beams afar
To fill the world with light.

—*William Cullen Bryant*

THE TRUTH IS WE CAN SEE WHAT WE NEED TO SEE BY STARLIGHT.

—*John Shea*

O morning stars, together proclaim the holy birth!
and praises sing to GOD the King,
and peace to men on earth.

—*Phillips Brooks*

The Friendly Beasts

Jesus our Brother, kind and good,
  Was humbly born in a stable rude,
    And the friendly beasts around Him stood;
      Jesus our Brother, kind and good.

"I," said the donkey, shaggy and brown,
  "I carried His mother up hill and down;
    I carried His mother to Bethlehem town.
      I," said the donkey, shaggy and brown.

"I," said the cow, all white and red,
  "I gave Him my manger for His bed;
    I gave Him my hay to pillow His head.
      I," said the cow, all white and red.

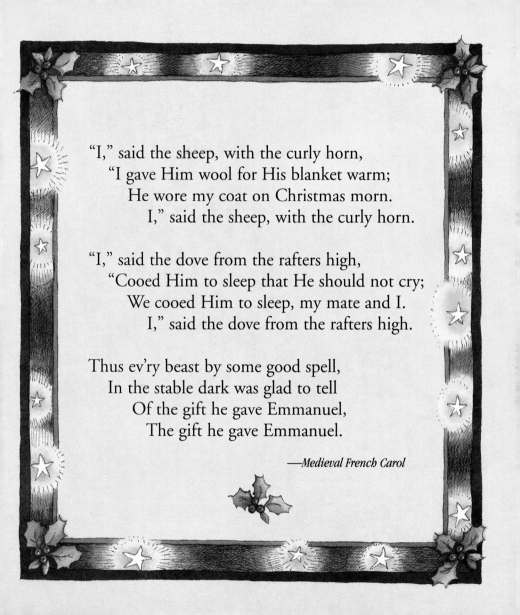

"I," said the sheep, with the curly horn,
  "I gave Him wool for His blanket warm;
    He wore my coat on Christmas morn.
      I," said the sheep, with the curly horn.

"I," said the dove from the rafters high,
  "Cooed Him to sleep that He should not cry;
    We cooed Him to sleep, my mate and I.
      I," said the dove from the rafters high.

Thus ev'ry beast by some good spell,
  In the stable dark was glad to tell
    Of the gift he gave Emmanuel,
      The gift he gave Emmanuel.

—*Medieval French Carol*

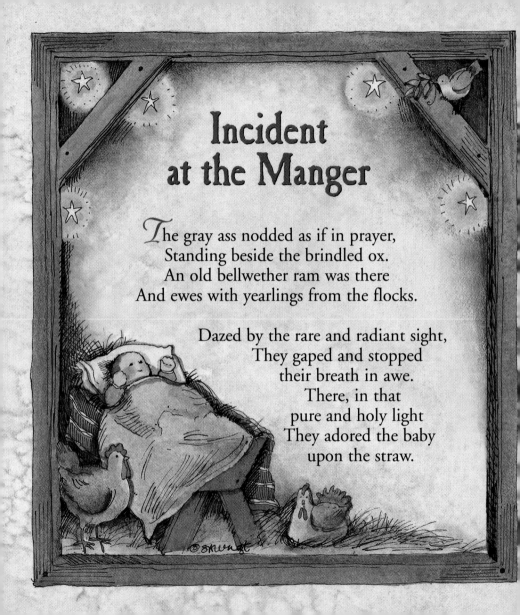

Incident
at the Manger

The gray ass nodded as if in prayer,
Standing beside the brindled ox.
An old bellwether ram was there
And ewes with yearlings from the flocks.

Dazed by the rare and radiant sight,
They gaped and stopped
their breath in awe.
There, in that
pure and holy light
They adored the baby
upon the straw.

A spotted pig stole out of the mist
And slipped past the ox and the ass unseen
And into the stable. The barnyard hissed,
"Go back to your mud hole! You're unclean."

He hoisted his rough, bewhiskered chin
Up onto the trough where the infant lay
(No easy thing for a fat boar's kin)
And peered at the child upon the hay.

Pig looked at baby wonderingly;
No creature whinnied or scoffed the while.
"Ox," said the ass, "Did I truly see?"
"Ass," said the ox, "Did the baby smile?"

—*C. W. Christian*
used with author permission

Sheep on the hillside lay whiter than snow;

Shepherds were watching them, long, long ago.

Glory to God in the Highest

There were some shepherds in that part of the country who were spending the night in the fields, taking care of their flocks. An angel of the Lord appeared to them, and the glory of the Lord shone over them. They were terribly afraid, but the angel said to them, *"Don't be afraid! I am here with good news for you, which will bring great joy to all the people. This very day in David's town your Savior was born—Christ the Lord! And this is what will prove it to you: You will find a baby wrapped in cloths and lying in a manger."*

Suddenly a great army of heaven's angels appeared with the angel, singing praises to God:

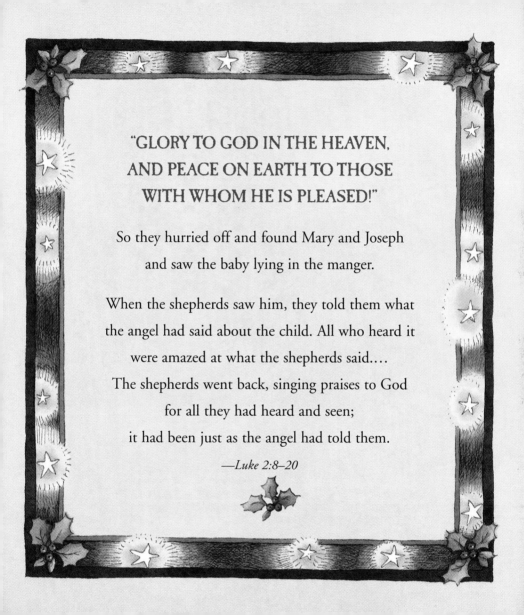

"GLORY TO GOD IN THE HEAVEN,
AND PEACE ON EARTH TO THOSE
WITH WHOM HE IS PLEASED!"

So they hurried off and found Mary and Joseph
and saw the baby lying in the manger.

When the shepherds saw him, they told them what
the angel had said about the child. All who heard it
were amazed at what the shepherds said....
The shepherds went back, singing praises to God
for all they had heard and seen;
it had been just as the angel had told them.

—*Luke 2:8–20*

*A*nd cradled there in the scented hay,
In the air made sweet by the breath of kine,
The little child in the manger lay,
The child, that would be king one day
Of a kingdom not human but divine.
His mother Mary of Nazareth
Sat watching beside his place of rest,
Watching the even flow of his breath,
For the joy of life and the terror of death
Were mingled together in her breast.

—Henry Wadsworth Longfellow

*T*HERE IS SUCH RICHNESS AND
GOODNESS IN THIS NATIVITY THAT
IF WE SHOULD SEE AND DEEPLY UNDERSTAND,
WE SHOULD BE DISSOLVED IN PERPETUAL JOY.

—Martin Luther
Translated by Roland H. Bainton

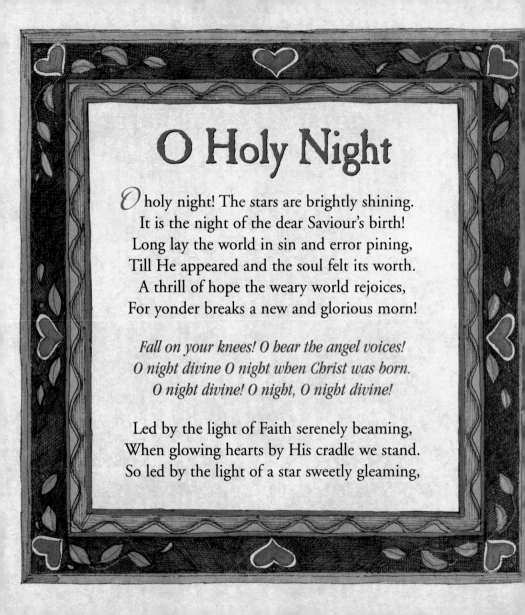

O Holy Night

O holy night! The stars are brightly shining.
It is the night of the dear Saviour's birth!
Long lay the world in sin and error pining,
Till He appeared and the soul felt its worth.
A thrill of hope the weary world rejoices,
For yonder breaks a new and glorious morn!

Fall on your knees! O hear the angel voices!
O night divine O night when Christ was born.
O night divine! O night, O night divine!

Led by the light of Faith serenely beaming,
When glowing hearts by His cradle we stand.
So led by the light of a star sweetly gleaming,

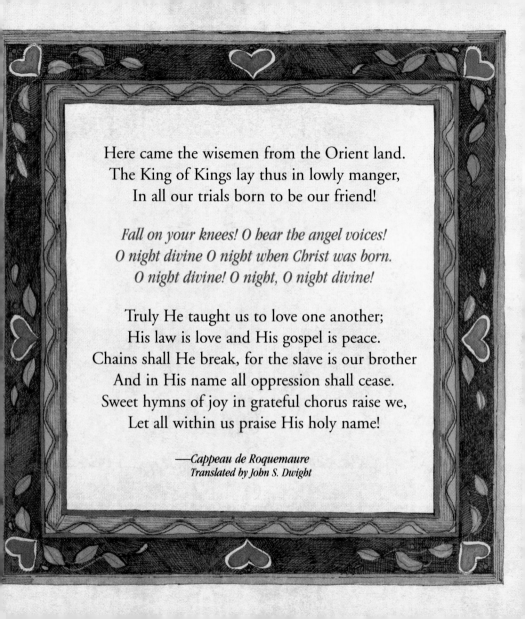

Here came the wisemen from the Orient land.
The King of Kings lay thus in lowly manger,
In all our trials born to be our friend!

Fall on your knees! O hear the angel voices!
O night divine O night when Christ was born.
O night divine! O night, O night divine!

Truly He taught us to love one another;
His law is love and His gospel is peace.
Chains shall He break, for the slave is our brother
And in His name all oppression shall cease.
Sweet hymns of joy in grateful chorus raise we,
Let all within us praise His holy name!

—*Cappeau de Roquemaure*
Translated by John S. Dwight

Angels!

From heaven high I come to you,
To bring you tidings strange and true.
Glad tidings of great joy I bring,
Whereof I now will say and sing.

To you this night is born a Child
Of Mary, chosen Mother mild;
This little Child, of lowly birth,
Shall be the joy of all the earth.

Glory to God in highest heaven,
Who unto us his Son hath given!
While angels sing with pious mirth,
A glad New Year to all the earth.

—Martin Luther
Translated by Catherine Winkworth

ALL MY HEART THIS NIGHT REJOICES, AS I HEAR, FAR AND NEAR, SWEETEST ANGEL VOICES; "CHRIST IS BORN," THEIR CHOIRS ARE SINGING, TILL THE AIR EVERYWHERE, NOW WITH JOY IS RINGING.

—*Paulus Gerhardt*
Translated by Catherine Winkworth

This lyrical beginning is heard
by the only ones who could hear it, the shepherds.
There is no hint here of the lyrics being heard
by any of the managers of the census.
They just kept counting.

—*Walter Breuggemann*

The Singing of Angels

There must be always remaining
in every man's life some place for the singing of angels—
some place for that which in itself is breathlessly beautiful
and by an inherent prerogative throwing all the rest of life
into a new and created relatedness. Something that gathers up
in itself all the freshest of experience from drab and commonplace areas of living and glows in one bright white light
of penetrating beauty and meaning—then passes.
The commonplace is shot through now with new glory—
old burdens become light, deep and ancient wounds lose much
of their old, old hurting. A crown is placed over our head
that for the rest of our lives we are trying
to grow tall enough to wear. Despite all of the
crassness of life, despite all of the hardness of
life, despite all the harsh discords of life,
life is saved by the singing of angels.

—Howard Thurman

What Child is This?

*W*hat Child is this who laid to rest
On Mary's lap is sleeping,
Whom angels greet with anthems sweet
While shepherds watch are keeping?
This, this is Christ the King
Whom shepherds guard and angels sing,
Haste, haste to bring Him laud,
The Babe, the Son of Mary.

Christmas Song

Oh raise your voices, shepherds low,
With those of glorious seraphim,
Join them in their thankful song,
This never-ending, joyous hymn.

For in a stable far away,
Among the ox and cooing dove
A holy babe is born today,
The only son of God above.

So come rejoicing one and all,
Come to Bethlehem and see
This holy infant, holy child,
And him adore on bended knee.

—*Elizabeth Buchanan*
used with author permission

They Followed The Star

Jesus was born in the town of Bethlehem in Judea, during the time when Herod was king. Soon afterward, some men who studied the stars came from the East to Jerusalem and asked, "Where is the baby born to be the king of the Jews? We saw his star when it came up in the east, and we have come to worship him."

When King Herod heard about this, he was very upset, and so was everyone else in Jerusalem. He called together all the chief priests and the teachers of the Law and asked them, "Where will the Messiah be born?"

"In the town of Bethlehem in Judea," they answered.
"For this is what prophet wrote: 'Bethlehem in the land of Judah,
you are by no means the least of the leading cities of Judah;
for from you will come a leader who will guide my people Israel.'"

So Herod called the visitors from the East to a secret meeting and found out from them the exact time the star had appeared. Then he sent them to Bethlehem with these instructions: "Go and make a careful search for the child; and when you find him, let me know, so that I too may go and worship him."

And so they left, and on their way they saw the same star they had seen in the East. When they saw it, how happy they were, what joy theirs! It went ahead of them until it stopped over the place where the child was. They went into the house, and when they saw the child with his mother Mary, they knelt down and worshiped him. They brought out their gifts of gold, frankincense, and myrrh, and presented them to him. Then they returned to their country by another road, since God had warned them in a dream not to go back to Herod.

—Matthew 2:1–12

The narrative of Luke paints for us a picture
of persons who were willing to look up in wonder
and to truly hear. Can we be such people as well?

—*Wendy M. Wright*

It is of profoundest significance to me that
the Gospel story, particularly in the Book of Luke,
reveals that the announcement of the birth of Jesus
comes first to simple shepherds who were about their
appointed tasks. After theology has done its work,
after the reflective judgments of men from the heights
and lonely retreats of privilege and security have wrought
their perfect patterns, the birth of Jesus remains the
symbol of the dignity and the inherent
worthfulness of the common man.

—*Howard Thurman*

Now one young shepherd was something of a cynic.
He whispered to his neighbor, "Is this real?
Am I drunk?" The other shepherd didn't answer.
He just pointed up at the sky.

—*Meg Crager*